WILFRED CAMPBELL

Selected Poems

With an Introduction
by
Carl F. Klinck

The Tecumseh Press
Ottawa - Canada
1976

Selection and Editorial Matter

© The Tecumseh Press Ltd. 1976.

ISBN 0-919662-57-9

The Tecumseh Press Limited
8 Mohawk Crescent
Ottawa
Canada.

Printed and bound in Canada.

CONTENTS

The Mind of Man

INTRODUCTION

Lake Lyrics

And store in my heart old music,
Melodies gathered and sung
By the genies of love and of beauty
When the heart of the world was young.
("Vapor and Blue")

Wilfred Campbell's use of the word "Lakes" is both general and specific. Sometimes he was referring to the vast system of inland freshwater seas named Ontario, Erie, Huron, Michigan and Superior, but more often mainly to the last three of these, "the upper," or northern, ones. Specifically, he described the grandeur and beauty of the lakes epitomized in the region around his home at Wiarton, Ontario.

This little settlement in the Indian country was most happily situated at the base of the Bruce Peninsula, which stretches seventy-five miles northward, partially dividing Georgian Bay from Lake Huron. On the edges of the Bay there are many minor inlets; the one at Wiarton is called Colpoy's. A striking feature of the town which has grown up there is the great limestone cliff, the first of the headlands looming majestically over fiords on the upward-tilted eastern side of the Peninsula. The western side appears to be tilted downwards into the beaches of Lake Huron: only seven miles west of Campbell's town stands Oliphant with its low, sandy shores and accessible islands. The poet, therefore, lived where the characteristic variety of the whole Great Lakes region, certainly that of the upper lakes, was conveniently and dramatically on display. In his day the shore-lines were still partially forest-rimmed, and there was still evidence of what they were like before the white man came.

William Wilfred had his first view of the waters of Georgian Bay, or rather of a long, sweeping south-eastern inlet of the Bay called Nottawasaga, when he arrived with his parents to live in Meaford, under the shadow of the Blue Mountains. He was then, in 1868, ten years of age: he had been born in Berlin (now Kitchener) in south-western Ontario on the 1st of June 1858. His father was an Anglican clergyman, a missionary who established congregations in various parts of Ontario before he took his family to Wiarton in 1872. This pioneer settlement was Wilfred's home during his most impressionable years (until he was twenty-two), while he was, successively, a freely-roving boy, a student at the Owen Sound High School (also in the lakeland), and a teacher at Zion in Kepple Township and at Purple Valley (near the Indian reservation at Cape Croker on the Peninsula).

There is no evidence to show that Wilfred wrote verse during this period: these years were given to the impact of natural objects upon the eye, the heart, and the memory. The emergence of verbal composition appeared when he enrolled at University College at Toronto in the autumn of 1880 and produced a variety of poems for publication in *The 'Varsity*, the university journal. Most of his Lake Lyrics, however, seem to have been composed, or at least polished, during the later 1880's while he was in the United States; and they were published in 1889 in St. John, New Brunswick. After a score of years he provided a prose commentary accompanying illustrations in a book entitled *The Canadian Lake Region* (1910).[1]

This carries one back to the source of his lake lyrics: the impact made upon him by beautiful and magnificent scenes, and the inevitable association of the waters and shores of the upper lakes with geological time, with the Indian era, and with modern man's precarious contact with immensity. "Even today," he wrote in 1910:[2]

in the twentieth century, out in their open spaces, . . . one still feels that great sense of loneliness and haunted solitude so pregnant with suggestions of the dim past which are so much associated with these vast inland waters. . . . where even the most modern steamer takes on suggestions of its environment; and mystery enwraps and dissolves the commonplace in its elusive folds of mist and sky-line.

Here even at mid-day in summer there are islands and lonely coves, as haunted and peopled with ghosts as grimmest midnight, so desolately remote is its whole atmosphere and spirit from all that is ephemeral and modern. It seems, at times, that this portion of our continent has thrown over it a spell of some enchantment laid by the peoples of the dim past who once dwelt here in the bygone ages; a spell which still lingers in the fitting environment of spectral water and fading, haze-wrapt shore.

The Indians of the Peninsula were often seen in Wiarton in Campbell's youth. Such proximity did little to dissipate the romance and mystery associated with their "dim past," although Wilfred's older brother Frank, a physician, had some communication with them and collected their relics, ornaments and legends. They were Chippewa (Ojibways) of the upper lakes, about whom Wilfred learned something by observation and report before he became acquainted (at what age one does not know) with the bookish compendium of Chippewa lore, Longfellow's *Hiawatha* (1855). "I was a child nurtured among the finer influences of music, culture, thought, and learning" he told an interviewer in his later life. Certainly there were books in the Campbell home, and it is difficult to believe that the popular *Hiawatha* was not among them. The Wiarton region also had legends of its own, attached to natural features such as the Indian "lover's leap" at Spirit Rock above the town; the curse of Manitou upon the "restless river"; and the "warriors eternally fixed in stone by Nana Boza to keep guard over the spirits of dead Indians." The great cliffs themselves were expressive of an Indian past, at Wiarton as well as at Manitoulin:[3]

All over-run with wild vines and creeping plants, these great masses of rock have the appearance and give the suggestion of old-world ruins, and the whole region bears about it a lonesome haunted air—suggesting some old association of life in those great, desolate spaces of shore and water.

Like a contemporary, Isabella Valancy Crawford, whose *Malcolm's Katie* is full of childhood memories of the pioneer village of Paisley (south of Wiarton), Campbell laid foundations for a mythology belonging to Ontario: subject matter, imagery, moods and structures appropriate to this part of the world.

The material for romance and mystery in the perennial catastrophies on the upper lakes was indigenous, however much it resembled events elsewhere:[4]

A storm on Lake Huron off the peninsula coast is terrific and grand in the extreme. Many wrecks have occurred for years back on these coasts, and a portion of the settlers at one time lived almost entirely upon the wreckage which came ashore from the pitiless, devouring lake.

As I quote these lines, I have before me a newspaper report of the sinking of a 709-foot ore carrier, the *Edmund Fitzgerald*, with twenty-nine crew members all lost, near Sault Ste. Marie, in the great storm of the 10th of November 1975.

By way of contrast, there is little originality in the short stories and abortive novels of hair-raising adventures, sensational incidents and two-dimensional characters which Campbell tried to place in magazines when he returned in 1890 for a seven-months' sojourn in the Lake Country at Southampton, on the shore of Lake Huron. These stories, evidently set in the Wiarton area, only hint at what sympathetic observation, naturalistic description, and adequate craftsmanship might have allowed him to contribute to the fiction of pioneer Ontario. He preferred, however, to imitate Mark Twain, Poe, Irving, and Dickens, succeeding only in leaving a piquant charm around real or invented place-names such as Big Hat, Wellington Sound, Northampton, Hadley's Island, Sandy Beach, Scratch's Point, Tranter's Cove, Mullet's Landing, Rat's Landing, Reef Settlement, Golden Valley, and Dog's Nest Corner.[5]

The composition of *Lake Lyrics* must be explained beyond origins in sense impressions: words, imagery, melody, and (conventional) forms came slowly to Campbell and chiefly later in periods of recollection. "Nama-Way-Qua-Donk—The Bay of Sturgeons" is the only poem which can be identified as "written in boyhood." It describes the bay at Wiarton, where the spirits of a wild and passionate Indian people linger nearby. *The 'Varsity* published it over the pseudonym of "Huron" a few months after Wilfred became a student in the college of arts at Toronto. Thus began a series of fifteen poems published in the university magazine from 1881 to 1883; but only two more, "Winter" and "The Love of Kewaydin," could be called Indian lake poems.

It is unlikely, therefore, that Wilfred arrived in Toronto with a large pack of "Huron" lyrics and ballads about the Lake country. He may have been modest about exposing his backwoods experience to academic critics, although he could have claimed a certain respect for his originality. It is still interesting to speculate why his spellings differ from Longfellow's. He had "Kewaydin" instead of the famous poet's "Keewaydin"; "Medwayosh" instead of "Mudwayauska"; and "Nama" instead of "Nahma." One of the contributions to *The 'Varsity*, however, the nature-poem called "Winter" ("From the cold and dreary northland"), is clearly an exercise in the rhythms of Longfellow's *Hiawatha*.

Most of the other poems published in the first *'Varsity* series were experiments in the melodies of Byron and Tennyson. They smelled of the academic lamp, rather than of northern winds. Only "Old Voices," "Autumn," "Orpheus" and "Rododactulos" were ever reprinted. Further conquests in sophisticated learning seemed possible for Campbell after he had demonstrated an artistic success in "Orpheus" and a classical flair in "Rododactulos." After a fruitful year of general studies in the University he transferred to Wycliffe, a neighbouring Anglican theological college, and then, in the autumn of 1883, to the Episcopal Theological School in Cambridge, Massachusetts.

He found this School happily situated near Harvard and actually next door to Craigie House, where Longfellow had lived. The famous poet had died in 1882, a year before Campbell arrived. During the two years of study which followed, the young student's mind and soul responded to the influences of this centre where studies in religion were supplemented by Longfellow's moral and religious songs. The divinity school's cherished independence, liberalism, and spirit of intelligent inquiry were not entirely lost on Campbell, but he was sceptical of reason, systematic religion, and, for the time being, of higher criticism. Doubtless he made good use of libraries whose stock of books surpassed any of his earlier resources. Through the courtesy of a friend, five of his poems were presented to W.D. Howells, who sent them to *The Atlantic Monthly*. "A Canadian Folk Song" was printed in the January 1885 issue of that magazine. Curiously, at this time, the effect upon Campbell of "culture", theology, and Longfellow resulted in the ambition to write domestic songs.

When he left Cambridge in 1885, he was called to minister to a congregation at West Claremont, New Hampshire. He served his parish in all kinds of weather; married a Canadian girl, and established a home, as he had seen his parents do in Wiarton. His own domestic life and rural surroundings reinforced his memories of boyhood and youth, and inspired a group of poems related either to the North or to New England, or as in "Snow" to both.

An extraordinary burst of publication began in 1886. The prestige of appearing in *The Atlantic* brought him access to the pages of *The Cottage Hearth* of Boston, *The New England*

Magazine and *The Magazine of American History*. In 1886–1888 the Toronto *'Varsity* also presented a new series of ten of Campbell's poems, including three lake lyrics: "Ballad of Lake Huron" [from which the lines of "Lake Huron, October" were later extracted], "The Flight of the Gulls," and "Manitou." *The American Magazine* published "The Legend of Dead Man's Lake."

The West Claremont years were evidently happy ones. Although the parish work was demanding, there was leisure. His congregation did not expect him to enter into theological subtleties: Christian love was the message of his sermons and also of poems like "Lazarus," "The Hebrew Father's Prayer," and "A Lyric of Love," which were later appended to *Lake Lyrics* (Part III). In these undated poems there is a new seriousness about despair, and about salvation through Love—sermonized obliquely in monologues. In "Ode to the Nineteenth Century," he strongly condemned "modern civilization" and called for a return to the moral visions of the "holier past." He began to see his vocation as a popular writer rather than as a priest.

He made a booklet of the domestic verse and called it *Snowflakes and Sunbeams*.[6] It was in print when he was welcomed back to Canada in September 1888 as rector at St. Stephen, New Brunswick. A larger anthology, composed of Lake Lyrics, Snowflakes and Sunbeams, and Other Poems was in view. Part I was still expanding: *The Century* magazine was publishing "The Winter Lakes" and "Vapor and Blue." The second of these poems became the "Prelude" to the handsome book, *Lake Lyrics and Other Poems* which came from the press of J. & A. McMillan of St. John in 1889 and received its first reviews in August.

It is almost beyond dispute that most of the lyrics of the Lakes were written in New England or at the international border at St. Stephen. The well-known "How One Winter Came in the Lake Region", printed in the March 1890 issue of *The Century*, was too late for this book and too early to be credited to Southampton on Lake Huron, whither Campbell moved in August or September of that year.

He did not settle down in Southampton, for he was planning a return to secular life. He had grown weary of parish routine, and his private struggle with rationalism was approaching a crisis which left him unable to defend doctrines of his Church. The growth of his doubts was reflected in the divisions which he made of the contents of *Lake Lyrics and Other Poems* in 1889; he had separated poems of the affections from the dramatizations of spiritual distress. It was indeed true that love was, and would remain, his subject—as he said in his "Invocation to the Lakes",

'tis love for God my heart hath quaffed,
And sympathy for man

but the "Parts" would differ: Part I expressed love of nature; Part II, love of home; and Part III, love on trial in his troubled mind. The next phase, love assailed by despair, would appear in *The Dread Voyage*, published in Toronto in 1893, two years after he had moved to Ottawa.

The Mind of Man

He arrived in Ottawa on the 18th of May 1891 to start work as an extra clerk in the civil service at a dollar and fifty cents a day. This was the best that Alexander McNeill, M.P., of Wiarton could do for him at the time. Campbell had given up, to use his own words in the Toronto *Globe*, "$1200 a year and a rectory to live a richer life at $500 a year." He was later refused an appointment to the Parliamentary Library, but on the 1st of June 1893 he began to work at a desk in the department of Militia and Defence. Archibald Lampman's job in the Post Office was probably comparable; Duncan Campbell Scott could look forward to greater advancement in Indian Affairs at Ottawa.

These two poets and Wilfred Campbell found literary relief in a column entitled *At the Mermaid Inn*, appearing in Saturday issues of *The Globe* from February 1892 until July 1893. Their essays were signed individually and this record of their critical opinions has merited reprinting in recent years. The conventional *Globe* was shocked when it discovered that it had given space, on the 27th of February 1892, to an article in which Campbell recommended John Fiske's writings on mythology and declared that "much of the earlier part of the Old Testament, such as the stories of the Garden of Eden, The Flood, The Serpent, the Story of Jonah, have all been proved to belong to the class of literature called mythic." "The story of the Cross itself," he had added, "is one of the most remarkable myths in the history of humanity; connected with the old phallic worship of some of our most remote ancestors." On Monday *The Globe* condemned such ideas, and Campbell published an explanation, which did not constitute a clear withdrawal. He seems to have held to his own faith in a religion of nature, "where the preachers are eternal, unconscious influences for ever at work," and to the adoption or creation of myth to illustrate what a man must do when nature's influences give no comfort.

A number of poems in *The Dread Voyage* (Toronto 1893) showed what he meant by "myth": these were principally "The Dread Voyage," "Unabsolved," "The Dreamers," "The Were-Wolves," and "The Mother." In such poems, mainly in the form of dramatic monologues, Campbell externalized his own depression and mental struggles as journeys into physical and sub-conscious horrors in an atmosphere of mystery and terrifying dead-ends. Some of his imagery recalled Coleridge, Poe and Browning.

"The Mother," published in *Harper's Monthly Magazine* in April 1891, will serve as an example of this new departure in Campbell's poetic expression. He had found his sources in a German legend mentioned by Edward B. Tylor in his *Primitive Culture* (1871).[7] John Fiske, a lecturer at Harvard, had quoted Tylor's story in his own book, *Myths and Mythmakers—Old Tales and Superstitions Interpreted by Comparative Mythology* (1872).[8] Campbell could not have been unaware that Fiske became one of the first writers to introduce "Darwinism" to American readers. Although Fiske stressed that Darwin's findings served to explain God's great design, Campbell was strongly moved to doubts about the supernatural and about eternal love. "The Mother," one observes, ends in a blank: the supreme myth of birth, life, love, struggle, death and revival is symbolized here only by death for the babe as well as the mother.

In this way Campbell reflected, not only the ultimate in his temporary surrender to rationalism, naturalism, and evolutionary theory, but also his adoption of Fiske's kind of "mythology" which used narrative means as outlets for some inner reaches of consciousness. There was something modern about this psychological approach, perhaps enough to gain recognition for Campbell now as a pioneer who anticipated in

Canada the various uses and refinements of myth by twentieth-century authors. When he achieved, as Roberts and Car-
man did, the neo-Greekish mythology of Mother Earth and
Kinship with the world of nature (distinctively employed by
the Confederation Poets), he had come by a road much
rougher than theirs to that reconciliation with Darwinism.

He was still inspired by ancient myth; to the early success
of "Orpheus" he now added such excellent poems as "Pan the
Fallen" and "Out of Pompeii." And he placed, side by side
with the stories of horror, lyrics which showed how eagerly he
still responded to nature's moods in spite of theories of her ind-
ifference to man. It appears that, in the winter of his discon-
tent at Southampton in 1890–1891, he composed some of his
most appreciative lyrics of the cold and stormy lakes. The
spring poems which followed promised recovery from depression.

So well did he recover that he dared to exploit his success
with dramatic monologues; he tried to write full-length
"closet" dramas. A half dozen poetic tragedies remain in
books and manuscripts as a largely unprofitable result of this
tremendous effort during the 1890's. The best of these plays
was *Mordred*, published along with *Hildebrand* in 1895.[9] It is
difficult now to read the rhetorical Tennysonian-Shakespea-
rean dramas into which Campbell poured so many of the fan-
cies and moral observations of his restless soul. And he still
had time for the many lyrics which would fill *Beyond the Hills
of Dream* (1899) and *The Collected Poems* (1905)!

Beyond the Hills of Dream was a critical edition, a collection
of his best poems primarily designed for magazine-trained
readers in the United States. It was attractively bound in soft
grey and ivory, lettered in gold, and smoothly named. But
what did the title mean? An answer depends on what he
meant by "dream." In one sense to "go beyond" was to put
behind himself the bad dreams of *The Dread Voyage* and to
come to "a world of fancy free"—probably the world of *Lake
Lyrics and Other Poems*:

Over the hills of care, my Love,
    Over the mountains of dread,
We come to a valley, glad and vast,
    Where we meet the long-lost dead;
And there the gods in splendour dwell,
    In a land where all is fair

> Over the mountains of dread, my Love,
> Over the hills of care.

Here "dream" means "pleasant memories" of people and joys of the Past. It was indeed a happy book, in which the belated monologue of "The Vengeance of Saki" is misplaced.

In 1905 William Briggs of Toronto published his *Collected Poems*, which (fortunately for the query about "dream") contained "Commemoration Ode," written by Campbell for the celebration of the twentieth anniversary of his class's graduation from the Episcopal Theological School. In the lines, and between them, one can assess what Cambridge had meant to him: first of all, "the olden faith in glad sincerity," reverence, wisdom, vision; later, evolutionary theory which he interpreted as "a grim dream of man's gross heredity"; and finally, enlightenment through the transcendental "dream" of Ralph Waldo Emerson. "Dream" and "Spirit" (or "soul") had become the key words in the Canadian poet's reconciliation of conflicting theories about nature and man.

He was ready to accept the view that the forms of nature and the spirit of man exist within the Whole in a harmony of "correspondences." "Dream" in this sense, therefore, is the word for insight, the wordless direct apprehension of kinship between "things" and man's spirit. This is how Campbell put it in his "Ode":[10]

> I have felt
> A sudden flame of some large knowledge flashed,
> And then withdrawn from out my spirit's ken;
> As though God opened His vast doors of light
> And outward being. Then my soul hath felt
> Some mystic glimpse of far infinity,
> As though there flamed a world outside our world,
> Beyond this prison-house of all our tears,
> This finite cell that we inhabit here.

In the sonnet "Morning" he uses the analogy of sunrise dissipating the "dreams and phantasies of pale distress" which night had brought. Nature, therefore, can be beneficent because of "correspondence" with the soul. In the *Collected* volume there are many other poems like "The Dryad's House" and "The Spring Spirit" which communicate the message of direct nature-man experience with admirable delicacy and subtlety. Campbell excelled, however, in occasional lines of imaginative expression rather than in whole poems.

10

Around the turn of the century he developed ambitions to be a public man as well as a poet. When Queen Victoria died and when the Boer War was in progress, he assumed the role of an unofficial poet laureate, first for Canada and then for the British imperial race.[11] "To the Canadian Patriot" is still one of our best patriotic poems. The contentious proposition that the British "race" had achieved the highest kind of morality to be found among the nations was behind all of his Imperialist exhortations. These verses evoke no interest now, although, in the history of Canadian literature, they are early twentieth-century examples of literature devoted to social and political matters. When Campbell went abroad in 1901, 1906, and 1911, they brought him favour in Britain. Since the personification of the "race" for Campbell was the Head of his clan, the Duke of Argyll, who had been Governor-General of Canada as Marquess of Lorne, the poet's Imperialism was not all patriotic rhetoric. Through personal friendship and hospitality at Inverary and elsewhere, the Duke gave substance to Imperial relations involving duties required of citizens in the new country as well as in the old.[12]

Like almost everything in Campbell's circle of affections, his Toryism involved a consistent attitude toward values derived from the past, and a desire to keep modern materialists from damaging civilization's inheritance. Among the manuscripts left unpublished at his death, there was a long prose treatise entitled "The Tragedy of Man" or "The Divine Origin of Man."[13] It was a summary of what he had been teaching in verse: the descent rather than the ascent of man; the "dual origin" of man as animal *and* spirit; and the moral superiority of the British race.

Four lines of "My Creed" had said most of this in shorter form:

This is my creed in face of cynic sneer,
The cavilling doubt, the pessimistic fear;—
We come from some far greatness, and we go
Back to a greatness, spite of all our woe.

His mass of evidence gathered from "ethnology, mythology, history, literature, archeology and development of civilization" will probably remain only in manuscript, but it lies behind his noblest and most imaginative poem, written on the 12th and 13th of April, 1910: "Stella Flamarum, An Ode to Halley's Comet."[14]

Little more needs to be said about his other prose works, except that *The Canadian Lake Region* (1910) is a useful supplement to the *Lake Lyrics*. *Canada* (1907), painted by T. Mower Martin and described by Campbell, was an earlier and more elegant production for an English market. Its illustrations are now collector's items. *The Scotsman in Canada*, Volume 1 (1912) was an uneven piece of research compiled by Campbell after he was promoted from the Privy Council Office to the Archives in 1908. His romances, a Scottish one called *Ian of the Arcades* (1906) and an Upper Canadian one called *A Beautiful Rebel* (1909) were pot-boilers, indicative only of the author's interest, if not skill, in historical narrative.

During the War of 1914–1918 he rendered all the service which he could as an older loyal civilian. He did not live to see the end of the conflict: he died on the morning of the first of January 1918. He was buried in peaceful Beechwood Cemetary in Ottawa, near the grave of Archibald Lampman, upon whose untimely death he had written the elegy, "Bereavement of the Fields."

Carl F. Klinck
University of Western Ontario

NOTES

1 Musson Book Company, Toronto.
2 *Ibid.*, 85.
3 *Ibid.*, 96.
4 *Ibid.*, 89.
5 Manuscripts at Queen's University, Kingston: *A Complete Bibliography (to 1940) of Wilfred Campbell*; is on file at Queen's University Library and at the University of Western Ontario (D.B. Weldon Library).
6 Reprinted in Ottawa, The Golden Dog Press, 1974.
7 "researches into the development of mythology, philosophy, religion, art and custom."
8 Fiske, pp. 229-230.
9 See *Poetical Tragedies* (Toronto: William Briggs, 1908) 316 pp.
10 [on cover] *The Collected Poems of Wilfred Campbell* (Toronto, 1905), pp. 35-38.
11 Carl F. Klinck, *Wilfred Campbell* (Toronto: Ryerson, 1942), p. 154.
12 *Ibid.*, pp. 152-213.
13 In Queen's University Library.
14 *Sagas of Vaster Britain* (London: Hodder & Stoughton, [1914]).

LAKE LYRICS

VAPOR AND BLUE

Domed with the azure of heaven,
　　Floored with a pavement of pearl,
Clothed all about with a brightness
　　Soft as the eyes of a girl,

Girt with a magical girdle,
　　Rimmed with a vapor of rest—
These are the inland waters,
　　These are the lakes of the west.

Voices of slumberous music,
　　Spirits of mist and of flame,
Moonlit memories left here
　　By gods who long ago came,

And vanishing left but an echo
　　In silence of moon-dim caves,
Where haze-wrapt the August night slumbers,
　　Or the wild heart of October raves.

Here where the jewels of nature
　　Are set in the light of God's smile;
Far from the world's wild throbbing,
　　I will stay me and rest me awhile.

And store in my heart old music,
　　Melodies gathered and sung
By the genies of love and of beauty
　　When the heart of the world was young.

TO THE LAKES

Blue, limpid, mighty, restless lakes,
　　God's mirrors underneath the sky,
Low rimmed in woods and mists, where wakes,
　　Through murk and moon, the marsh bird's cry.

Where ever on, through drive and drift,
 'Neath blue and grey, through hush and moan,
Your ceaseless waters ebb and lift
 Past shores of century-crumbling stone.

And under ever-changing skies,
 Swell, throb, and break on kindling beach;
Where fires of dawn responsive rise,
 In answer to your mystic speech.

Past lonely haunts of gull and loon,
 Past solitude of land-locked bays,
Whose bosoms rise to meet the moon,
 Beneath their silvered film of haze.

Where mists and fogs in ghostly bands,
 Vague, dim, moon-clothed in spectral light;
Drift in from far-off haunted lands,
 Across the silences of night.

THE WINTER LAKES

Out in a world of death far to the northward lying,
 Under the sun and the moon, under the dusk and the day,
Under the glimmer of stars and the purple of sunsets dying;
 Wan and waste and white, stretch the great lakes away.

Never a bud of spring, never a laugh of summer,
 Never a dream of love, never a song of bird;
But only the silence and white, the shores that grow chiller
  and dumber,
  Wherever the ice winds sob, and the griefs of winter are
  heard.

Crags that are black and wet out of the gray lake looming,
 Under the sunset's flush and the pallid, faint glimmer of
  dawn;

Shadowy, ghost-like shores, where midnight surfs are boom-
      ing
   Thunders of wintry woe over the spaces wan.

Lands that loom like specters, whited regions of winter,
   Wastes of desolate woods, deserts of water and shore;
A world of winter and death, within these regions who enter,
   Lost to summer and life, go to return no more.

Moons that glimmer above, waters that lie white under,
   Miles and miles of lake far out under the night;
Foaming crests of waves, surfs that shoreward thunder,
   Shadowy shapes that flee, haunting the spaces white.

Lonely hidden bays, moon-lit, ice-rimmed, winding,
   Fringed by forests and crags, haunted by shadowy shores;
Hushed from the outward strife, where the mighty surf is
      grinding
   Death and hate on the rocks, as sandward and landward
      it roars.

MORNING ON THE BEACH

(Lake Huron, June)

See the night is beginning to fail,
   The stars have lost half of their glow;
As though all the flowers in a garden did pale,
   When a rose is beginning to blow.

And the breezes that herald the dawn,
   Blown round from the caverns of day;
Lift the film of dark from the heavens bare lawn,
   Cool and sweet as they come up this way.

And this mighty swayed bough of the lake
   Rocks cool where the morning hath smiled;
While the dim, misty dome of the world scarce awake
   Blushes rose, like the cheek of a child.

THE HEART OF THE LAKES

There are crags that loom like spectres
    Half under the sun and the mist;
There are beaches that gleam and glisten,
There are ears that open to listen,
    And lips held up to be kissed.

There are miles and miles of waters
    That throb like a woman's breast,
With a glad harmonious motion
    Like happiness caught at rest,
As if a heart beat under
    In love with its own glad rest;
Beating and beating forever,
    Outward to east and to west.

There are forests that kneel forever,
    Robed in the dreamiest haze
That God sends down in the summer
    To mantle the gold of its days,
Kneeling and leaning forever
    In winding and sinuous bays.

There are birds that like smoke drift over,
    With a strange and bodeful cry,
Into the dream and the distance
    Of the marshes that southward lie,
With their lonely lagoons and rivers,
    Far under the reeling sky.

HOW SPRING CAME

(To the Lake Region)

No passionate cry came over the desolate places,
    No answering call from iron-bound land to land;
But dawns and sunsets fell on mute, dead faces,
    And noon and night death crept from strand to strand.

18

'Til love breathed out across the wasted reaches,
   And dipped in rosy dawns from desolate deeps;
And woke with mystic songs the sullen beaches,
   And flamed to life the pale, mute, death-like sleeps.

Then the warm south, with amorous breath inblowing,
   Breathed soft o'er breast of wrinkled lake and mere;
And faces white from scorn of the north's snowing,
   Now rosier grew to greet the kindling year.

LAKE HURON

(October)

Miles and miles of lake and forest,
   Miles and miles of sky and mist,
Marsh and shoreland where the rushes
   Rustle, wind and water kissed;
Where the lake's great face is driving,
   Driving, drifting into mist.

Miles and miles of crimson glories,
   Autumn's wondrous fires ablaze;
Miles of shoreland red and golden,
   Drifting into dream and haze;
Dreaming where the woods and vapors,
   Melt in myriad misty ways.

Miles and miles of lake and forest,
   Miles and miles of sky and mist,
Wild birds calling where the rushes
   Rustle, wind and water kissed;
Where the lake's great face is driving,
   Driving, drifting into mist.

ON THE LEDGE

I lie out here on a ledge with the surf on the rocks below me,
The hazy sunlight above and the whispering forest behind;
I lie and listen, O lake, to the legends and songs you throw me,
Out of the murmurous moods of your multitudinous mind.

I lie and listen a sound like voices of distant thunder,
The roar and throb of your life in your rock wall's mighty
  cells;
Then after a softer voice that comes from the beaches under,
A chiming of waves on rocks, a laughter of silver bells.

A glimmer of bird-like boats, that loom from the far horizon;
That scud and tack and dip under the gray and the blue;
A single gull that floats and skims the waters, and flies on
Till she is lost like a dream, in the haze of the distance, too.

A steamer that rises a smoke, then after a tall, dark funnel,
That moves like a shadow across your water and sky's gray
  edge;
A dull, hard beat of a wave that diggeth himself a tunnel,
Down in the crevices dark under my limestone ledge.

And here I lie on my ledge, and listen the songs you sing
  me,
Songs of vapor and blue, songs of island and shore;
And strange and glad are the hopes and sweet are the
  thoughts you bring me,
Out of the throbbing depths and wells of your heart's great
  store.

ODE TO THE LAKES

(In June)

O magic region of blue waters throbbing,
  O blown wave-garden, 'neath the north world's span;
Wild paradise, girt in by crag-walls, robbing
  All earth of beauty since the world began,

I dream again your voice of beaches sobbing
　　And crave a boon more sweet than gift of man;—

Once more in the ripe heart of golden summer,
　　To drift upon your blue pearled wimpling breast;
To watch God's dawn, bud, bloom, a flushed incomer,
　　To see him die with flames in thy hushed west;
To even know the entranced silence dumber,
　　Because of heart awe-hushed and lips love-pressed.

To watch the dimmed day deepen into even,
　　The flush of sunset melt in pallid gold;
While the pale planets blossom out in heaven;
　　To feel the under silence trance and hold
The night's great heartbeats; soul-washed, nature-shriven,
　　To feel the mantle of silence fold and fold.

To know the horologe of nature timing
　　The dawning or the golden heart of noon,
To hear in spirit magic bells set chiming
　　On silver continents of the rising moon;
To read in sky, wave, wood, God's poet rhyming
　　In mystic rhythm nature's eternal rune.

And so forget the sorrow and the glory,
　　The passion and the pain that men call life;
To let the past go like a long-told story,
　　The long-forgotten and the long-dead strife;
But just to drift here while the years grow hoary,
　　Dead to earth's living with all its anguish rife.

And know no voice save that of beaches chanting,
　　No eye save June's own glorious dome of blue;
And so be dead to all the strife and canting,
　　The violence of souls that were untrue;
And only know one love, the mighty panting
　　Of your great heart that throbs your being through.

ODE TO THUNDER CAPE

Storm-beaten cliff, thou mighty cape of thunder;
Rock-Titan of the north, whose feet the waves beat under;
Cloud-reared, mist-veiled, to all the world a wonder,
Shut out in thy wild solitude asunder,
   O Thunder Cape, thou mighty cape of storms.

About thy base, like wo that naught assuages,
Throughout the years the wild lake raves and rages;
One after one, time closes up weird pages;
But firm thou standest, unchanged, through the ages,
   O Thunder Cape, thou awful cape of storms.

Upon thy ragged front, the storm's black anger,
Like eagle clings, amid the elements' clangor:
About thee feels the lake's soft sensuous languor;
But dead alike to loving and to anger,
   Thou towerest bleak, O mighty cape of storms.

Year in, year out, the summer rain's soft beating,
Thy front hath known, the winter's snow and sleeting;
But unto each thou givest contemptuous greeting.
These hurt thee not through seasons fast and fleeting;
   O proud, imperious, rock-ribbed cape of storms.

In August nights, when on thy under beaches,
The lake to caverns time-wierd legend teaches;
And moon-pearled waves to shadowed shores send
   speeches,
Far into heaven, thine awful darkness reaches,
   O'ershadowing night; thou ghostly cape of storms.

In wild October, when the lake is booming
Its madness at thee, and the north is dooming
The season to fiercest hate, still unconsuming,
Over the strife, thine awful front is looming;
   Like death in life, thou awful cape of storms.

Across thy rest the wild bee's noonday humming,
And sound of martial hosts to battle drumming,
Art one to thee—no date knows thine incoming;

The earliest years belong to thy life's summing,
    O ancient rock, thou aged cape of storms.

O thou so old, within thy sage discerning,
What sorrows, hates, what dead past loves still-burning,
Couldst thou relate, thine ancient pages turning;
O thou, who seemest ever new lores learning,
    O unforgetting, wondrous cape of storms.

O tell me what wild past lies here enchanted:
What borders thou dost guard, what regions haunted?
What type of man a little era flaunted,
Then passed and slept? O tell me thou undaunted,
    Thou aged as eld, O mighty cape of storms.

O speak, if thou canst speak, what cities sleeping?
What busy streets? what laughing and what weeping?
What vanished deeds and hopes like dust unheaping,
Hast thou long held within thy silent keeping?
    O wise old cape, thou rugged cape of storms.

These all have passed, as all that's living passes;
Our thoughts they wither as the centuries' grasses,
That bloom and rot in bleak, wild lake morasses:
But still thou loomest where Superior glasses
    Himself in surge and sleep, O cape of storms.

And thou wilt stay when we and all our dreaming
Lie low in dust. The age's last moon-beaming
Will shed on thy wild front its final gleaming;
For last of all that's real and all that's seeming,
    Thou still wilt linger, mighty cape of storms.

THE TIDES OF DAWN

How cool across the lake's pearled, heaving floor,
   The spirit winds of morning steal in here:
   Dim mists of darkness rise from marsh and mere,
And pallid phantoms brood at morning's door.
Beyond yon east the surfs of dawning roar,
   To break in flame-waves on night's sombre beach;
   The heart still hears their impetuous, golden speech,
Imploring morn the daylight to restore.

Soon, soon, across the night's gray, ruined walls,
   Will flood and surge the crimson tides of morn;
   Bathing the east and all the dusks forlorn;
Soon, soon, across the dawn's white silence falls
   Glory and music, morning's song and fire:
   The waking world leaps to the day's desire.

CRAGS

Gaunt, huge, misshapen, 'neath the northern night,
   These wild lake crags loom black against the sky,
   While at their feet the restless waters sigh
And beat and moan amid the fitful light.
Here no life comes or takes its shadowy flight,
   No voice save winds that shoreward faint and die;
   But ever through their weird rifts tow'ring high,
The moon with ray of gold the lake doth smite.

Men call them warrior-souls to adamant turned
Doomed through these thousand years that since have
    burned,
   To guard the prisoned souls that wander here;
So, dead to hate and waste, the centuries' storms,
True to their trust, they lift their awful forms,
   And keep these passes bleak, these regions drear.

MEDWAYOSH

A world of dawn, where sky and water merge
  In far, dim vapors, mingling blue in blue,
    Where low-rimmed shores shimmer like gold shot
      through
Some misty fabric. Lost in dreams, I urge
With languid oar my skiff through sunny surge,
  That rings its music round the rocks and sands,
  Passing to silence, where far lying lands
Loom blue and purpling from the morning's verge.

I linger in dreams, and through my dreaming comes,
Like sound of suffering heard through battle drums,
  An anguished call of sad, heart-broken speech;
As if some wild lake spirit, long ago
Soul-wronged, through hundred years its wounded woe
  Moans out in vain across each wasted beach.

SNOW

Down out of heaven,
  Frost-kissed
And wind driven,
  Flake upon flake,
  Over forest and lake,
Cometh the snow.

Folding the forest,
  Folding the farms,
In a mantle of white;
  And the river's great arms,
Kissed by the chill night
  From clamor to rest,
Lie all white and shrouded
  Upon the world's breast.

Falling so slowly
  Down from above,
So white, hushed, and holy,
  Folding the city
Like the great pity
  Of God in His love;
Sent down out of heaven
  On its sorrow and crime,
Blotting them, folding them
  Under its rime.

Fluttering, rustling,
  Soft as a breath,
The whisper of leaves,
  The low pinions of death,
Or the voice of the dawning,
  When day has its birth,
Is the music of silence
  It makes to the earth.

Thus down out of heaven,
  Frost-kissed
And wind-driven,
  Flake upon flake,
Over forest and lake,
  Cometh the snow.

LITTLE BLUE EYES AND GOLDEN HAIR

Little blue eyes and golden hair
Sits like a fairy beside my chair,
And gazes with owlish look on the fire,
Where the great log crackles upon his pyre;
And down in my heart there broods a prayer—
God bless blue eyes and golden hair.

Little blue eyes and golden hair
Chatters and laughs and knows no care;
Though far outside the night is bleak,

And under the eaves the shrill winds shriek
And rattle the elm boughs chill and bare—
God bless blue eyes and golden hair.

Little blue eyes and golden hair,
Taken all sudden and unaware,
Caught in the toils of the drowsy god,
Has gone on a trip to the Land of Nod;
Half fallen in my lap she lies,
With a warp of dreams in her lash-hid eyes;
And deep in my heart still broods that prayer—
God bless blue eyes and golden hair.

A WINTER'S NIGHT

Shadowy white,
Over the fields are the sleeping fences,
Silent and still in the fading light,
As the wintry night commences.

The forest lies
On the edge of the heavens, bearded and brown;
He pulls still closer his cloak, and sighs,
As the evening winds come down.

The snows are wound
As a winding sheet on the river's breast,
And the shivering blast goes wailing round,
As a spirit that cannot rest.

Calm sleeping night!
Whose jewelled couch reflects the million stars
That murmur silent music in their flight—
O, naught thy fair sleep mars.

And all a dream—
Thy spangled forest in its frosty sleep,
Thy pallid moon that sheds its misty beam,
And looming wraiths that o'er the moorlands creep.

As through the night
The trailing snows winds as a funeral train,
   And softly through the murky morning light
The dim grey day comes stealing up again.

INDIAN SUMMER

Along the line of smoky hills
   The crimson forest stands,
And all the day the blue-jay calls
   Throughout the autumn lands.

Now by the brook the maple leans
   With all his glory spread,
And all the sumachs on the hills
   Have turned their green to red.

Now by great marshes wrapt in mist,
   Or past some river's mouth,
Throughout the long, still autumn day
   Wild birds are flying south.

RODODACTULOS

The night blows outward in a mist,
And all the world the sun has kissed.

Along the golden rim of sky,
A thousand snow-piled vapors lie.

And by the wood and mist-clad stream,
The Maiden Morn stands still to dream.

AN AUGUST REVERIE

There is an autumn sense subdues the air,
   Though it is August and the season still
A part of summer, and the woodlands fair.
   I hear it in the humming of the mill,
I feel it in the rustling of the trees,
That scarcely shiver in the passing breeze.

'Tis but a touch of Winter ere his time,
   A presaging of sleep and icy death,
When skies are rich and fields are in their prime,
   And heaven and earth commingle in a breath:—
When hazy airs are stirred with gossamer wings,
And in shorn fields the shrill cicada sings.

So comes the slow revolving of the year,
   The glory of nature ripening to decay,
When in those paths, by which, through loves austere,
   All men and beasts and blossoms find their way,
By steady easings of the Spirit's dream,
From sunlight past the pallid starlight's beam.

Nor should the spirit sorrow as it passes,
   Declining slowly by the heights it came;
We are but brothers to the birds and grasses,
   In our brief coming and our end the same:
And though we glory, godlike in our day,
Perchance some kindred law their lives obey.

There are a thousand beauties gathered round:
   The sound of waters falling over-night,
The morning scents that steam from the fresh ground,
   The hair-like streaming of the morning light
Through early mists and dim, wet woods where brooks
Chatter, half-seen, down under mossy nooks.

The ragged daisy starring all the fields,
   The buttercup abrim with pallid gold,
The thistle and burr-flowers hedged with prickly shields,
   All common weeds the draggled pastures hold,
With shriveled pods and leaves, are kin to me,
Like-heirs of earth and her maturity.

They speak a silent speech that is their own,
    These wise and gentle teachers of the grass;
And when their brief and common days are flown,
    A certain beauty from the year doth pass:—
A beauty of whose light no eye can tell,
Save that it went; and my heart knew it well.

I may not know each plant as some men know them,
    As children gather beasts and birds to tame;
But I went 'mid them as the winds that blow them,
    From childhood's hour, and loved without a name.
There is more beauty in a field of weeds
Than in all blooms the hothouse garden breeds.

For they are nature's children; in their faces
    I see that sweet obedience to the sky
That marks these dwellers of the wilding places,
    Who with the season's being live and die;
Knowing no love but of the wind and sun,
Who still are nature's when their life is done.

They are a part of all the haze-filled hours,
    The happy, happy world all drenched with light,
The far-off, chiming click-clack of the mowers,
    And yon blue hills whose mists elude my sight;
And they to me will ever bring in dreams
Far mist-clad heights and brimming rain-fed streams.

In this dream August air, whose ripened leaf,
    Pausing before it puts death's glories on,
Deepens its green, and the half-garnered sheaf
    Gladdens the haze-filled sunlight, love hath gone
Beyond the material, trembling like a star
To those sure heights where all thought's glories are.

And Thought, that is the greatness of this earth,
    And man's most inmost being, soars and soars,
Beyond the eye's horizon's outmost girth,
    Garners all beauty, on all mystery pores:—
Like some ethereal fountain in its flow,
Finds heavens where the senses may not go.

HOW ONE WINTER CAME
IN THE LAKE REGION

For weeks and weeks the autumn world stood still,
   Clothed in the shadow of a smoky haze;
The fields were dead, the wind had lost its will,
And all the lands were hushed by wood and hill,
   In those grey, withered days.

Behind a mist the blear sun rose and set,
   At night the moon would nestle in a cloud;
The fisherman, a ghost, did cast his net;
The lake its shores forgot to chafe and fret,
   And hushed its caverns loud.

Far in the smoky woods the birds were mute,
   Save that from blackened tree a jay would scream,
Or far in swamps the lizard's lonesome lute
Would pipe in thirst, or by some gnarlèd root
   The tree-toad trilled his dream.

From day to day still hushed the season's mood,
   The streams stayed in their runnels shrunk and dry;
Suns rose aghast by wave and shore and wood,
And all the world, with ominous silence, stood
   In weird expectancy:

When one strange night the sun like blood went down,
   Flooding the heavens in a ruddy hue;
Red grew the lake, the sere fields parched and brown,
Red grew the marshes where the creeks stole down,
   But never a wind-breath blew.

That night I felt the winter in my veins,
   A joyous tremor of the icy glow;
And woke to hear the north's wild vibrant strains,
While far and wide, by withered woods and plains,
   Fast fell the driving snow.

THE MYSTERY

What is this glory nature makes us feel,
And riots so sweet within us? Can it be
That there with man is kindred mystery
Of being, old heredity
Of bud and leaf, of pulsing plant and tree,
And earth and air; that in some olden speech,—
Ere words had being—doth our spirits reach:
Some essence akin to music, subtle, deep,
That plumbs our souls as dreams melt through our sleep?

Yea, it must be: for often unto me
A fallen leaf hath greater power to stir
Than mighty volumes of earth's history,
Or all the tragedy of life's great blur.
What is it? that so little; plant or flower,
A sunset or a sunrise, gives us wings,
Or opens doors of glory every hour,
To godlike thoughts—and life's imaginings.
Yea, 'tis a greatness that about us lies;
Within our touch—pervading air and sod,
That bounds our being—hidden from our eyes
But inward, subtle,—linking life to God.

SANCTUARY

All the long years I have wandered wide,
    But now I am going home;
Far from the restless, seething tide,
    From the fever of hearts that roam;
Far from the streets of oppression and pride,
    From the helot hate and·hire,
To the sunset lands of eventide,
    The home of the heart's desire.

There in the great lake country,
Walled in from the world's mad dreams;
Its envies, its joy that seems;
  Its loves, its hates, and its tears;
To lie and sleep where the sun drinks deep,
  Through the golden slumber of years.

You had my heart from the first;
  And there would I lie at the last,
When the fever and fret that cursed,
  And the long heartache had passed;
To sleep through the long, long sleep,
  When the eye may see no more;
At home and one with wind and sun,
  In your glory of haze and shore.

THE MIND OF MAN

LAZARUS

O, Father Abram, I can never rest,
   Here in they bosom in the whitest heaven,
   Where love blooms on through days without an even;
   For up through all the paradises seven,
There comes a cry from some fierce, anguished breast.

A cry that comes from out of hell's dark night,
   A piercing cry of one in agony,
   That reaches me here in heaven white and high;
   A call of anguish that doth never die;
Like dream-waked infant wailing for the light.

O, Father Abram, heaven is love and peace,
   And God is good; eternity is rest.
   Sweet would it be to lie upon thy breast
   And know no thought but loving to be blest
Save for that cry that never more will cease.

It comes to me above the angel-lyres,
   The chanting praises of the cherubim;
   It comes between my upward gaze and Him,
   All-blessed Christ. A voice from the vague dim,
"O, Lazarus, come and ease me of these fires."

"O, Lazarus, I have called thee all these years,
   It is so long for me to reach to thee,
   Across the ages of this mighty sea,
   That loometh dark, dense, like eternity;
Which I have bridged by anguished prayers and tears.

"Which I have bridged by knowledge of God's love,
   That even penetrates this anguished glare;
   A gleaming ray, a tremulous, star-built stair,
   A road by which love-hungered souls may fare
Past hate and doubt, to heaven and God above."

So calleth it ever upward unto me.
   It creepeth in through heaven's golden doors,
   It echoes all along the saphire floors,
   Like smoke of sacrifice, it soars and soars,
It fills the vastness of eternity.

Until my sense of love is waned and dimmed,
  The music-rounded spheres do clash and jar,
  No more those spirit-calls from star to star,
  The harmonies that float and melt afar,
The belts of light by which all heaven is rimmed.

No more I hear the beat of heavenly wings,
  The seraph chanting in my rest-tuned ear;
  I only know a cry, a prayer, a tear,
  That rises from the depths up to me here;
A soul that to me suppliant leans and clings.

O, Father Abram, thou must bid me go
  Into the spaces of the deep abyss;
  Where far from us and our God-given bliss,
  Do dwell those souls that have done Christ amiss;
For through my rest I hear that upward wo.

I hear it crying through the heavenly night,
  When curvéd, hung in space, the million moons
  Lean planet-ward, and infinite space attunes
  Itself to silence, as from drear grey dunes,
A cry is heard along the shuddering light,

Of wild dusk-bird, a sad, heart-curd'ling cry,
  So comes to me that call from out hell's coasts;
  I see an infinite shore with gaping ghosts;
  This is no heaven, with all its shining hosts;
This is no heaven until that hell doth die.

So spake the soul of Lazarus, and from thence,
  Like new-fledged bird from its sun-jewelled nest,
  Drunk with the music of the young year's quest;
  He sank out into heaven's gloried breast,
Spaceward turned, toward darkness dim, immense.

Hellward he moved like radiant star shot out
  From heaven's blue with rain of gold at even',
  When Orion's train and that mysterious seven
  Move on in mystic range from heaven to heaven.
Hellward he sank, followed by radiant rout.

The liquid floor of heaven bore him up,
  With unseen arms, as in his feathery flight,
  He floated down toward the infinite night;
  But each way downward, on the left and right,
He saw each moon of heaven like a cup

Of liquid, misty fire that shone afar
  From sentinel towers of heaven's battlements;
  But onward, winged by love's desire intense,
  And sank, space-swallowed, into the immense.
While with him ever widened heaven's bar.

'Tis ages now long-gone since he went out,
  Christ-urged, love-driven, across the jasper walls,
  But hellward still he ever floats and falls,
  And ever nearer come those anguished calls;
And far behind he hears a glorious shout.

POETRY

Earth's dream of poetry will never die.
It lingers while we linger, base or true—
A part of all this being. Life may change,
Old customs wither, creeds become as nought,
Like autumn husks in rainwinds; men may kill
All memory of the greatness of the past,
Kingdoms may melt, republics wane and die,
New dreams arise and shake this jaded world;
But that rare spirit of song will breathe and live
While beauty, sorrow, greatness hold for men
A kinship with the eternal; until all
That earth holds noble wastes and fades away.
Wrong cannot kill it. Man's material dream
May scorn its uses, worship baser hope
Of life's high purpose, build about the world
A brazen rampart: through it all will come
The iron moan of life's unresting sea;
And through its floors, as filtered blooms of dawn,

Those flowers of dream will spring, eternal, sweet,
Speaking for God and man; the infinite mystery
Will ever fold life round; the mighty heart
Of earth's humanity ceaseless throb and beat
As round this globe the vasty deeps of sky,
And round earth's shores the wide, encompassing sea.
Outside this rind of hardened human strife
There lies this mantle of mighty majesty,
Thought's cunning cannot probe, its science plumb.
Earth's schools of wisdom, in their darkness, spell
The common runes of knowledge; but there lies
A greatness, vast, behind this taper gleam,
That stands for somewhat lore hath never weighed
In all its ponderings of thought-pulsing brain.
Shakespeare, the Mighty, touched it as he passed.
The Man in Uz did feel it, shook the folds
Of some great garment's hem of One who passed
The vasty gates of Orion at one stride.
All earth's high souls have felt it in their time,
Have risen to this mighty deep in thought,
Or worshipped in the blackness and the gleam.

Dream not because life's taper flame grows dim,
Man's soul grows wasted gazing on dull gold,
His spirit shrunk with canker of life's ill,
That earth's great nights will darken their splendors down,
Her dawns will fail to rise, this mighty world
Will cease to roll its vast appointed way;
And beauty and love, and all that man holds sweet
For youth and age, the effort glad, the joy,
The memory of old greatness gone before,
Not hold their magic 'neath the Almighty Will.

Yea, 'tis eternal as the wave, the sky,
Changing forever, never wholly passing,
A part of all this dream that will not die,
It lives forever. Years may fade and pass,
Youth's dream decline to age and death's decay,
Ills and sharp griefs, despairs and agonies come:
While earth remains her spirit will not fail.
That greatness back of all will still console,
Man's life will still be sweet, its purpose glad,

The morn will still be morning, and the night
Star splendors arched above the eternal peace,
The eternal yearning and the eternal dream.

LINES ON A SKELETON

This was the mightiest house that God e'er made,
This roofless mansion of the incorruptible.
These joists and bastions once bore walls as fair
As Solomon's palace of white ivory.
Here majesty and love and beauty dwelt,
Shakespeare's wit from these lorn walls looked down.
Sadness like the autumn made it bare,
Passion like a tempest shook its base,
And joy filled all its halls with ecstasy.

This was the home wherein all dreams of earth
And air and ocean, all supreme delights,
Made mirth and madness: wisdom pored alone;
And power dominion held: and splendid hope:
And fancy like the delicate sunrise woke
To burgeoning thought and form and melody.
Beneath its dome the agony of the Jew,
The pride of Caesar or the hate of Cain,
The thought of Plato or the heart of Burns
Once dwelt in some dim form of being's light.

Within these walls of wondrous structure, dread,
A magic lute of elfin melody
Made music immortal, such as never came
From out those ancient halls of Orphean song.

Love dreamed of it, and like a joy it rose.
Power shaped its firm foundations like the base
Of mountain majesty: and o'er its towers
Truth from fair windows made his light look down.

But came a weird and evil demon host,
Beseiged its walls, destroyed its marvellous front;
Shuttered its casements, dismantled all its dream,
And hurled it down from out its sunward height;
And now it lies bereft of all its joy
And pride and power and godlike majesty;
The sport of elements and hideous mimes,
That blench its corridors, desecrate its rooms,
Where once dwelt love and beauty, joy and hope,
Now tenantless: save for the incurious wind,
And ghostlike rains that beat its bastions bare,
And evil things that creep its chambers through.

But whither thence is fled that tenant rare,
That weird indweller of this wasted house?
Back from the petalled bloom withdraws the dew,
The melody from the shell, the day from heaven,
To build afar earth's resurrection morn.

And so, Love trusts, in some diviner air
The lord of this lorn mansion dwells in light
Of vaster beauty, vaster scope and dream;
Where weariness and gladness satiate not,
Where power and splendid being know no ruin,
And evil greeds and envyings work no wrong.

MY CREED

This is my creed in face of cynic sneer,
The cavilling doubt, the pessimistic fear;—
We come from some far greatness, and we go
Back to a greatness, spite of all our woe.

MORNING

When I behold how out of ruined night
Filled with all weirds of haunted ancientness,
And dreams and phantasies of pale distress,
Is builded, beam by beam, the splendid light,
The opalescent glory, gem bedight,
Of dew-emblazoned morning; when I know
Such wondrous hopes, such luminous beauties grow
From out earth's shades of sadness and affright;

O, then, my heart, amid thy questioning fear,
Dost thou not whisper: He who buildeth thus
From wrecks of dark such wonders at his will,
Can re-create from out death's night for us
The marvels of a morning gladder still
Than ever trembled into beauty here?

THE DREAM DIVINE

Who hath no moods for beauty doth not know
The inward greatness of this moving world.
My heart was troubled with the care of life
And mine own driven nature, when I came
Out to a place where 'mid the roofs of trees,
A single gleam, the evening sky shone through
In simple beauty, and it seemed as though
Once more as in the child-like olden days
When earth's folk dreamed God'd windows opened wide
And let in heaven. Thus it seemed to me,
For on my soul a sweetness and a calm
Fell like a mantle; and the joy of one
Who hearkens to inward music; all the world
Seemed in an instant changed: the garish streets
Were no more common; even the woes of men
Assumed a greatness, and mine own dread care
Grew dim, remote, a part of yesterday.

It is a marvel how this magic works,
That nature hath such influence over men,
To raise them from the common, and redeem
The soul from sordid evils, lift to beauty,
Build o'er our life a splendid weft of dream,
By one small rift of dawn or night divine.

THE DISCOVERERS

This poem is dedicated to the memory of all those great souls who,
in days gone by, in the bold spirit of discovery ventured out on the
then trackless seas of the unknown west, in quest of this New World
which their undaunted zeal and enterprise have won for us as a boon
to the race and a blessing to mankind.

They feared no unknown, saw no horizon dark,
Counted no danger; dreamed all seas their road
To possible futures: struck no craven sail
For sloth or indolent cowardice; steered their keels
O'er crests of heaving ocean, leagues of brine,
While Hope firm kept the tiller, Faith, in dreams,
Saw coasts of gleaming continents looming large
Beyond the ultimate of the sea's far rim.
Thus was it ever. Souls too great for sloth
And impotent ease, goaded by inward pain
Of some divine, great yearning restlessness;
Which would not sit at home on servile shores
And take the good their fathers wrought in days
Long-ancient time-ward,—reap what others sowed;
But nobler, sought to win a world their own,
Not conquered by others, but a virgin shore,
Where men might build the future; rear new realms
Of human effort; forgetful of the past,
And all its ill and failure; raising anew
The godlike dreams of genius, knowing only
Immortal possibility of man
To grow to larger vastness, holier dreams,
Made certain in straight laws of human life
And national vision; lived in lofty lives
Of manhood strong and noblest womanhood.

So thus it was, and is, and e'er will be!
The ill we do we leave behind us as
The phantom cloak of yesterday's sleep, thrown off
At newer waking to life's splendid dawn.
So dreamed they, eager, in those olden days,
Saw visions in the future, round the west
Of Europe's fading sunsets; held a hope
Of some new paradise for poor men's cure
From despotisms of old dynasties
And cruel iron creeds of warped despairs.
Hungering for light and truth and righteousness,
So launched they, setting sail toward sunset verge
Of lonely, inhospitable Ocean hurling back
From his grey mane sad wrecks of their desires.

We know their story, read the truth where they
Knew only in man's hope and loftier soul
Which strove and dared and greatly overcame,
Conquering scorn of man and veils of doubt,
Wrestling from nature half her secret, cruel,
Wherewith she darkens down in glooms apart
The mystery of this planet, where we sleep
And wake and toil, redeeming high resolves,
Chaining the future to the present act.

We ponder on their daring, their vast hope,
That compassed all a planet in its dream.
We marvel at that stern defiance, where
A single man, in a degenerate age,
Would throw the gauntlet down against a world,
Defying narrow custom, small beliefs,
Strangled in lies; and staking all on one
Swift certainty of reason, based on thought,
Which read from nature, not from childish tomes
Of baseless superstitions, and dared all,
Left the kind land behind, and ventured out
On what men deemed a hideous demon waste,
An endless vortex, wherein poor souls caught
Were swept to vastness, gulfed and swallowed down.
We wonder at this greatness, yet we know
That thus forever shall human greatness be,
Man's only truth in life to stand alone;
Invincible power the spirit's solitude.

45

Beneath the sky, that marvel of earth's night,
That vast reproof of all our littleness,
That shining rebuke to our unfaithfulness,
That scorner of our despairs; 'neath its dim tent
Of fold on fold of fleecy infinities;
That soul of man is but a puny thing,
A fork-like snake in its own petty fires,
Which doth not rise to some high eminence
Of human thought and vast forgetfulness
Of all this common ill and common deed,
And loom to somewhat of that stature, great,
That God did dream us! So those mighty souls,
Watching His stars, read nightly fixed and sure,
A certainty; while every yeasty wave,
A monster mountain, roared to gulf them down.

We are a part of that great dream they dreamed.
We know wherein they failed, as all life fails.
We know the greatness they could never dream,
The certainty behind that sunset veil,
Which lured them on beyond its misty verge;
And we are witness that their hope was sure,
And true and wise and voice of God to men.

We are the witnesses that they were right,
And all the small and common minds were wrong,
The scorners of their faith, the laughers-down
Of their sublime enthusiasms; like as all
Dim ages of this world have heard and seen.

Yea, we are witnesses that they who hoped,
And greatly planned, and greatly dreamed and dared,
Were greater and more god-like, truer souls
And wiser in their day than those who sat
With shaking head and shallow platitude,
Made foolish vulgar prophecy of defeat;
Yea, we are witnesses that one true man
With faith in nature, his own heart and brain,
And daring, fearless, caring nought for aught,
Save his own trust in some high godlike vision,
Is greater far than all a world of men
Who are but shadows of a worn-out age

Which they have long outlived; as rotten trunks
Do mark the place where some huge oak went down.

We are the dream which they did dream; but we,
If we are great as they were, likewise know
That man is ever onward, outward bound
To some far port of his own soul's desire,
Knowing the present ever incomplete,
In love's reflection of the heart's high goal.

And now no more this western world is deemed
A home for liberty and hope's desire.
Men learn in wisdom, as the years glide on,
And life is ever the same in east or west.
And human nature, lost in its own toils
Of earthly striving, loses that gold thread
Of life's sincerity, repeating o'er again
The grim despotic tyrannies of old,
On newer shores to freedom dedicate
By loftier souls who won this world in vain.

So is it ever. Human grief and ill
And human tyranny know no special strand.
All lands alike to tyrants are a spoil,
From ills of race no continent is immune.
Men cannot flee old evils though they cross
Whole oceans of surges beating in between.
We bear with us the despot in our blood:
It is the race that speaks forever in
Our strivings and our weakness: Nero flames
A newer Rome in each new tyranny
Which wakens a western world to deeds of blood.

And we, who have no continents new to find,
No shadowed planet darkening back our dream,
Who know the new world but the old world new:
The same old evil and the same old gleam
In other guise; but 'neath the same snakehead,
Lifting ill eyes to choke our visions down
In monster folds of human servitude:—
We, too, as they, are earth's discoverers,
We likewise can be fixed in our regard,

We likewise can be brave, sincere and true,
Dreaming far peaks of greatness on ahead,
If we but strive and beat our weakness down;
Setting our sails, invincible, for those ports
Beyond the common, sheltered shoals of self;
Cleaving with daring keel those open seas
Of larger life, those heaving floors of hope;
Marking our course by those fixed stars alone,
Forever steadfast, witnesses of God,
Pointing to continents vast of holier dream.

BEREAVEMENT OF THE FIELDS

(In Memory of Archibald Lampman, who died
February 10th, 1899)

Soft fall the February snows, and soft
Falls on my heart the snow of wintry pain;
For never more, by wood or field or croft,
Will he we knew walk with his loved again;
No more, with eyes adream and soul aloft,
In those high moods where love and beauty reign,
Greet his familiar fields, his skies without a stain.

Soft fall the February snows, and deep
Like downy pinions from the moulting breast
Of the all-mothering sky, round his hushed sleep,
Flutter a million loves upon his rest,
Where once his well-loved flowers were fain to peep,
With adder-tongue and waxen petals prest,
In young spring evenings reddening down the west.

Soft fall the February snows, and hushed
Seems life's loud action, all its strife removed,
Afar, remote, where grief itself seems crushed,
And even hope and sorrow are reproved;
For he whose cheek erstwhile with hope was flushed,
And by the gentle haunts of being moved,
Hath gone the way of all he dreamed and loved.

Soft fall the February snows, and lost,
This tender spirit gone with scarce a tear,
Ere, loosened from the dungeons of the frost,
Wakens with yearnings new the enfranchised year,
Late winter-wizened, gloomed, and tempest-tost;
And Hesper's gentle, delicate veils appear,
When dream anew the days of hope and fear.

And Mother Nature, she whose heart is fain,
Yea, she who grieves not, neither faints nor fails,
Building the seasons, she will bring again
March with rudening madness of wild gales,
April and her wraiths of tender rain,
And all he loved,—this soul whom memory veils,
Beyond the burden of our strife and pain.

Not his to wake the strident note of song,
Nor pierce the deep recesses of the heart,
Those tragic wells, remote, of might and wrong;
But rather, with those gentler souls apart,
He dreamed like his own summer days along,
Filled with the beauty born of his own heart,
Sufficient in the sweetness of his song.

Outside this prison-house of all our tears,
Enfranchised from our sorrow and our wrong,
Beyond the failure of our days and years,
Beyond the burden of our saddest song,
He moves with those whose music filled his ears,
And claimed his gentle spirit from the throng,—
Wordsworth, Arnold, Keats, high masters of his song.

Like some rare Pan of those old Grecian days,
Here in our hours of deeper stress reborn,
Unfortunate thrown upon life's evil ways,
His inward ear heard ever that satyr horn
From Nature's lips reverberate night and morn,
And fled from men and all their troubled maze,
Standing apart, with sad, incurious gaze.

And now, untimely cut, like some sweet flower
Plucked in the early summer of its prime,
Before it reached the fullness of its dower,

He withers in the morning of our time;
Leaving behind him, like a summer shower,
A fragrance of earth's beauty, and the chime
Of gentle and imperishable rhyme.

Songs in our ears of winds and flowers and buds
And gentle loves and tender memories
Of Nature's sweetest aspects, her pure moods,
Wrought from the inward truth of intimate eyes
And delicate ears of him who harks and broods,
And, nightly pondering, daily grows more wise,
And dreams and sees in mighty solitudes.

Soft fall the February snows, and soft
He sleeps in peace upon the breast of her
He loved the truest; where, by wood and croft,
The wintry silence folds in fleecy blur
About his silence, while in glooms aloft
The mighty forest fathers, without stir,
Guard well the rest of him, their rare sweet worshipper.

AFTERGLOW

After the clangor of battle
There comes a moment of rest,
And the simple hopes and the simple joys
And the simple thoughts are best.

After the victor's paean,
After the thunder of gun,
There comes a lull that must come to all
Before the set of the sun.

Then what is the happiest memory?
Is it the foe's defeat?
Is it the splendid praise of a world
That thunders by at your feet?

Nay, nay, to the life-worn spirit
The happiest thoughts are those
That carry us back to the simple joys
And the sweetness of life's repose.

A simple love and a simple trust
And a simple duty done,
Are truer torches to light to death
Than a whole world's victories won.

OUT OF POMPEII

She lay, face downward, on her bended arm,
　　In this her new, sweet dream of human bliss,
Her heart within her fearful, fluttering, warm,
　　Her lips yet pained with love's first timorous kiss.
She did not note the darkening afternoon,
　　She did not mark the lowering of the sky
O'er that great city. Earth had given its boon
　　Unto her lips, love touched her and passed by.

In one dread moment all the sky grew dark,
　　The hideous rain, the panic, the red rout,
Where love lost love, and all the world might mark
　　The city overwhelmed, blotted out
Without one cry, so quick oblivion came,
　　And life passed to the black where all forget;
But she—we know not of her house or name—
　　In love's sweet musings doth lie dreaming yet.

The dread hell passed, the ruined world grew still,
　　And the great city passed to nothingness:
The ages went and mankind worked its will.
　　Then men stood still amid the centuries' press,
And in the ash-hid ruins opened bare,
　　As she lay down in her shamed loveliness,
Sculptured and frozen, late they found her there,
　　Image of love 'mid all that hideousness.

Her head, face downward, on her bended arm,
　　Her single robe that showed her shapely form,

Her wondrous fate love keeps divinely warm
  Over the centuries, past the slaying storm;
The heart can read in writings time hath left,
  That linger still through death's oblivion;
And in this waste of life and light bereft,
  She brings again a beauty that had gone.

And if there be a day when all shall wake,
  As dreams the hoping, doubting human heart,
The dim forgetfulness of death will break
  For her as one who sleeps with lips apart;
And did God call her suddenly, I know
  She'd wake as morning wakened by the thrush,
Feel that red kiss across the centuries glow,
  And make all heaven rosier by her blush.

THE MOTHER

This poem was suggested by the following passage in Tyler's Animism:
"The pathetic German superstition that the dead mother's coming
back in the night to suckle the baby she has left on earth may be
known by the hollow pressed down in the bed where she lay".

I

It was April, blossoming spring,
They buried me, when the birds did sing;

Earth, in clammy wedging earth,
They banked my bed with a black, damp girth.

Under the damp and under the mould
I kenned my breasts were clammy and cold.

Out from the red beams, slanting and bright,
I kenned my cheeks were sunken and white.

I was a dream, and the world was a dream,
And yet I kenned all things that seem.

52

I was a dream, and the world was a dream,
And yet I kenned all things that seem.

I was a dream, and the world was a dream,
But you cannot bury a red sunbeam.

For though in the under-grave's doom-night
I lay all silent and stark and white,

Yet over my head I seemed to know
The murmurous moods of wind and snow,

The snows that wasted, the winds that blew,
The rays that slanted, the clouds that drew

The water-ghosts up from lakes below,
And the little flower-souls in the earth that grow.

Under earth, in the grave's stark night,
I felt the stars and the moon's pale light.

I felt the winds of ocean and land
That whispered the blossoms soft and bland.

Though they had buried me dark and low,
My soul with the season's seemed to grow.

II

From throes of pain they buried me low,
For death had finished a mother's woe.

But under the sod, in the grave's dread doom,
I dreamed of my baby in glimmer and gloom.

I dreamed of my babe, and I kenned that his rest
Was broken in wailings on my dead breast.

I dreamed that a rose-leaf hand did cling:
Oh, you cannot bury a mother in spring!

When the winds are soft and the blossoms are red
She could not sleep in her cold earth-bed.

I dreamed of my babe for a day and a night,
And then I rose in my graveclothes white.

I rose like a flower from my damp earth-bed.
To the world of sorrowing overhead.

Men would have called me a thing of harm,
But dreams of my babe made me rosy and warm.

I felt my breasts swell under my shroud;
No star shone white, no winds were loud;

But I stole me past the graveyard wall,
For the voice of my baby seemed to call;

And I kenned me a voice, though my lips were dumb:
Hush, baby, hush! for mother is come.

I passed the streets to my husband's home;
The chamber stairs in a dream I clomb;

I heard the sound of each sleeper's breath,
Light waves that break on the shores of death.

I listened a space at my chamber door,
Then stole like a moon-ray over its floor.

My babe was asleep on a stranger arm,
"O baby, my baby, the grave is so warm,

"Though dark and so deep, for mother is there!
O come with me from the pain and care!

"O come with me from the anguish of earth,
Where the bed is banked with a blossoming girth,

"Where the pillow is soft and the rest is long,
And mother will croon you a slumber-song—

"A slumber-song that will charm your eyes
To a sleep that never in earth-song lies!

"The loves of earth, your being can spare,
But never the grave, for mother is there."

I nestled him soft to my throbbing breast,
And stole me back to my long, long rest.

And here I lie with him under the stars,
Dead to earth, its peace and its wars;

Dead to its hates, its hopes, and its harms,
So long as he cradles up soft in my arms.

And heaven may open its shimmering doors,
And saints make music on pearly floors,

And hell may yawn to its infinite sea,
But they never can take my baby from me.

For so much a part of my soul he hath grown
That God doth know of it high on His throne.

And here I lie with him under the flowers
That sun-winds rock through the billowy hours,

With the night-airs that steal from the murmuring sea,
Bringing sweet peace to my baby and me.

PAN THE FALLEN

He wandered into the market
    With pipes and goatish hoof;
He wandered in a grotesque shape,
    And no one stood aloof.
For the children crowded round him,
    The wives and greybeards, too,
To crack their jokes and have their mirth,
    And see what Pan would do.

The Pan he was they knew him,
    Part man, but mostly beast,
Who drank, and lied, and snatched what bones
    Men threw him from their feast;
Who seemed in sin so merry,
    So careless in his woe,
That men despised, scarce pitied him,
    And still would have it so.

He swelled his pipes and thrilled them,
    And drew the silent tear;
He made the gravest clack with mirth
    By his sardonic leer.
He blew his pipes full sweetly
    At their amused demands,
And caught the scornful, earth-flung pence
    That fell from careless hands.

He saw the mob's derision,
    And took it kindly, too,
And when an epithet was flung,
    A coarser back he threw;
But under all the masking
    Of a brute, unseemly part,
I looked, and saw a wounded soul,
    And a godlike, breaking heart.

And back of the elfin music,
    The burlesque, clownish play,
I knew a wail that the weird pipes made,
    A look that was far away,—
A gaze into some far heaven
    Whence a soul had fallen down;
But the mob only saw the grotesque beast
    And the antics of the clown.

For scant-flung pence he paid them
    With mirth and elfin play,
Till, tired for a time of his antics queer,
    They passed and went their way;
Then there in the empty market
    He ate his scanty crust,

And, tired face turned to heaven, down
   He laid him in the dust.

And over his wild, strange features
   A softer light there fell,
And on his worn, earth-driven heart
   A peace ineffable.
And the moon rose over the market,
   But Pan the beast was dead;
While Pan the god lay silent there,
   With his strange, distorted head.

And the people, when they found him,
   Stood still with awesome fear.
No more they saw the beast's rude hoof,
   The furtive, clownish leer;
But the lightest spirit in that [throng]
   Went silent from the place,
For they knew the look of a god released
   That shone from his dead face.

TO THE CANADIAN PATRIOT

This is the land of the rugged North; these wide,
Life-yielding fields, these inland oceans; these
Vast rivers moving seaward their wide floods,
Majestic music: these sky-bounded plains
And heaven-topping mountains; these iron shores,
Facing toward either ocean; fit home, alone,
For the indomitable and nobly strong.

In that dread hour of evil when thy land
Is rent with strifes and ground with bigotry,
And all looks dark for honor, and poor Truth
Walks cloaked in shadow, alien from her marts,
Go forth alone and view the earth and sky,
And those eternal waters, moving, vast,
In endless duty, ever rendering pure
Those mild or angry airs; the gladdening sun,

Reviving, changing, weaving life from death;
Those elemental uses nature puts
Her patient hours to; and then thou shalt know
A larger vista, glean a greater truth
Than man has put into his partial creeds
Of blinded feud and custom. Thou wilt know
That nature's laws are greater and more sure,
More calm, more patient, wise and tolerant,
Than these poor futile efforts of our dream;
That human life is stronger in its yearning
Than those blind walls our impotence builds between;
And underneath this calloused rind we see,
As the obedient tides the swaying moon,
A mightier law the whole wide world obeys,
And far beyond these mists of human vision
God's great horizon stands out fixed and sure.

STELLA FLAMMARUM

An Ode to Halley's Comet

Strange wanderer out of the deeps,
    Whence, journeying, come you?
From what far, unsunned sleeps
    Did fate foredoom you,
Returning for ever again,
    Through the surgings of man,
A flaming, awesome portent of dread
    Down the centuries' span?

Riddle! from the dark unwrung
    By all earth's sages;—
God's fiery torch from His hand outflung,
    To flame through the ages;
Thou Satan of planets eterne,
    'Mid angry path,
Chained, in circlings vast, to burn
    Out ancient wrath.

By what dread hand first loosed

From fires eternal?
With majesties dire infused
  Of force supernal,
Takest thy headlong way
  O'er the highways of space?
O wonderful, blossoming flower of fear
  On the sky's far face!

What secret of destiny's will
  In thy wild burning?
What portent dire of humanity's ill
  In thy returning?
Or art thou brand of love
  In maskings of bale?
And bringest thou ever some mystical surcease
  For all who wail?

Perchance, O Visitor dread,
  Thou hast thine appointed
Task, thou bolt of the vast outsped!
  With God's anointed,
Performest some endless toil
  In the universe wide,
Feeding or curing some infinite need
  Where the vast worlds ride.

Once, only once, thy face
  Will I view in this breathing;
Just for a space thy majesty trace
  'Mid earth's mad seething;
Ere I go hence to my place,
  As thou to thy deeps,
Thou flambent core of a universe dread,
  Where all else sleeps.

But thou and man's spirit are one,
  Thou poet! thou flaming
Soul of the dauntless sun,
  Past all reclaiming!
One in that red unrest,
  That yearning, that surge,
That mounting surf of the infinite dream,
  O'er eternity's verge.